A Sanctuary
FOR YOUR Soul

KAY ARTHUR

INTERIORS BY
ANN PLATZ

HARVEST HOUSE PUBLISHERS
EUGENE, OREGON 97402

A Sanctuary for Your Soul

Copyright © 1999 by Kay Arthur
Published by Harvest House Publishers
Eugene, Oregon 97402

Library of Congress Cataloging-in-Publication Data

Arthur, Kay, 1933–
    A sanctuary for your soul / Kay Arthur
      p.   cm.
    ISBN 1–56507–946–9
    1. Women—Religious life. 2. Home—Religious
aspects—Christianity. 3. Arthur, Kay, 1933–   .   I. Title.
BV4527.A78—1998
242'.643—dc21   98–14674
                                        CIP

Photography of Ann Platz's mountain home
by Ronnie Owings of Pro Studio, Morrow, Georgia

Design and production by Koechel Peterson & Associates,
Minneapolis, Minnesota

Printed in the United States of America.

99 00 01 02 03 04 05 06 07 08 / BG / 10 9 8 7 6 5 4 3 2 1

Come away, my beloved . . .

Inside, there's a longing...

the sweet nostalgia that draws you

to a haven of your own...

a place called home.

This is your domain...

where you can enter in, shut the door,

and choose what...

when...

where...

God is LOVE

A refuge of your creation...
A home in process...an expression of you.

A sanctuary you can create,
A harbor of safety for loved ones
from the storms of life,
Your shelter in the world
—from the world.
A sanctuary for your soul.

This is part of the joy, the wonder, of being a woman. Here you celebrate the expression of being you as you take a house and make it your home. What you create in your setting makes it uniquely you.

And over the years, as you acquire with patience,

one well-chosen treasure at a time,

you're designing a memory of you

your loved ones will cherish,

a memory of a place you made home.

Maybe you are only able to
begin with a corner,
but you begin...
a special picture, a pretty cup
and saucer, a soft throw—
things that warm and delight
and nurture your soul.

This can be your place to run to...

to retreat to...

to call your own.

Your haven, where you can dream, reflect, replenish, restore.

It's the simple things you do that bring

satisfaction to your soul...

that delight the eyes...

that speak in the beauty of silence...

A vase filled with Queen Anne's
lace gathered from a field,
   Daisies or black-eyed Susans
from beside the road,
   A winter's branch crafted by
summer's sun and stormy winds,

And finally the smallest of bottles, vases, or pitchers

cradling violets, yellow buttercups, or tiny buds

nestled among a small sprig of baby's breath.

These are the brushstrokes of your

loving artistry on the canvas of your home...

Lights brought low,

Flickering candles soften the room,

creating the warmth you so desire...

a sense of security.

The sweet fragrance calling from the kitchen,

A table lovingly prepared...
You have created a gracious setting for this special time,
An interlude in your day.
Now around your table loved ones can safely talk and tell,

listen and laugh,

engage and enjoy,

rehearse and reflect on the day...

Because you have fashioned a setting,

an atmosphere for strengthening relationships,

for forming character.

An occasion to restore the graciousness of living.

You're building memories...
For them and for you...
Memories that will endure
the times of separation,
and nurture them with
the security of family.

Like the fragrance of a delightful potpourri,
    your sanctuary is filled with the scent of a woman.
For, in large portion, the presence of you,
    the essence of you,
    permeates and sets the atmosphere
    of this place called home.

You know, for you've watched the power
of a gentle smile,
of a non-condemning, listening ear,
of open, forgiving arms,
of your words and tone of voice,

the mystical effect of a soft answer that turns away wrath,

the power of words of kindness and encouragement

when they grace your lips...

It brings the same feelings of comfort, safety,

and security as turning

on soft lights in a favorite room—

    although some things are well-worn with time,

there's a warmth, a coziness, a sense of the familiar
in the shadow of night.

As you walk through your home,

turning out the lights, closing another day,

there's a sense of satisfaction, of accomplishment,

as you give one last, loving touch,

putting away the remnants of the day...

knowing that with everything in place,

when you awake you can begin with a

sense of peace and grace.

Your home has become a sanctuary,

a place of order.

There's a deep sense of contentment,

of accomplishment,

For you've looked well to the ways

of your household, your home.

Now is your time to nurture your soul...
Time to relax, to be blessedly quiet, to think...
about where you're going,
what really is important...
Time to separate the precious from the worthless,
the holy from the mundane...

Time to consider your ways...your future...

Time to plan what you want

for your loved ones...

to create for those you hold dear,

a sense of the spiritual,

a sense of security,

that which is necessary to sustain this sanctuary,

to keep it more than a house—

to make it a home,

a haven they're drawn to.

You can be at peace,

have contentment in your soul,

a spiritual thirst quenched...

an inner longing satisfied.

For in your home,

that corner that is yours,

is a place to deepen your faith,

to be still and commune with the One who knows you,

the Creator of your soul.

Peace be to you and peace be

to your house, and peace

be to all you have.

1 Samuel 25:6